Photogems

A Devotional

GREG W. DAVIS

Photogems

A Devotional

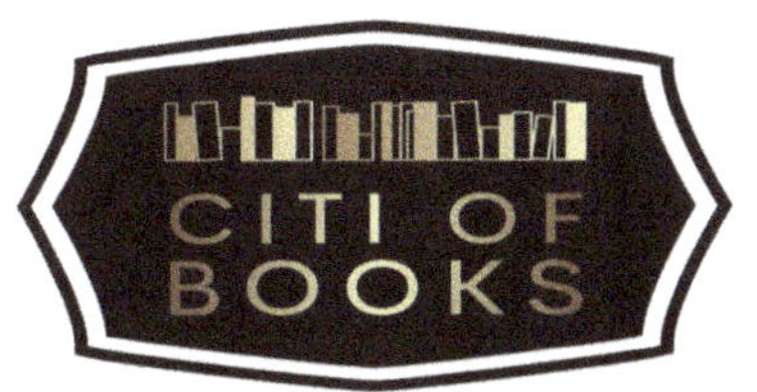

CITIOFBOOKS, INC.
3736 Eubank NE Suite A1
Albuquerque, NM 87111-3579
www.citiofbooks.com
Hotline: 1 (877) 389-2759
Fax: 1 (505) 930-7244

Ordering Information:
Quantity sales. Special discounts are available on quantity purchases by corporations, associations, and others. For details, contact the publisher at the address above.

Printed in the United States of America.

ISBN-13: Softcover   978-1-959682-57-8
          Hardcover   978-1-962366-60-1
          eBook   978-1-959682-58-5

Library of Congress Control Number: 2022922684

D
Dedication

A special thank-you to my daily inspiration, Jesus Christ, as well as my wife, Julia R. Davis (my Gem), and my children Dawn, and Haley, my congregation, DeKalb United Pentecostal Church, as well as my treasured friends, Robert and Anne Frake, St. Paul, MN, who requested we author this book.

Notes

Preface

When I was in college, in St. Paul, Minnesota, in 1981, I was required to take a class, that has changed my life. It was called ***Prayer Principals*** taught by Mrs. Ruth Foster. Mrs. Foster was a quiet, lovely lady, who daily displayed Christian virtue in so many inspiring ways. Her brother, President of the College had given her a difficult class to teach to over 300 students who already "thought" they knew everything about prayer and devotional already in their young lives. Week by week, Mrs. Foster began to uncover our woeful deficiencies with her self-deprecating humor and firm requirements for daily devotion and prayer. The principals she revealed through the Holy Spirit altered the way I thought of myself, my God, and my faith. May the thoughts that Scripture brings to your mind, do the same for you.

Greg W. Davis, *Author*

Notes

Contents

Notes

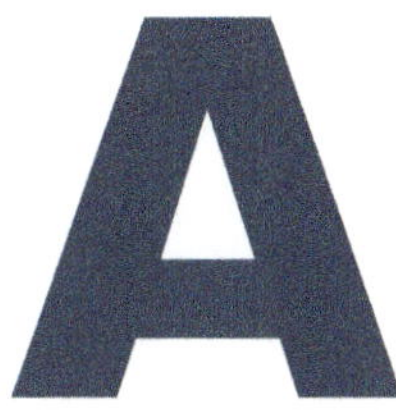

A

An Unfading Crown

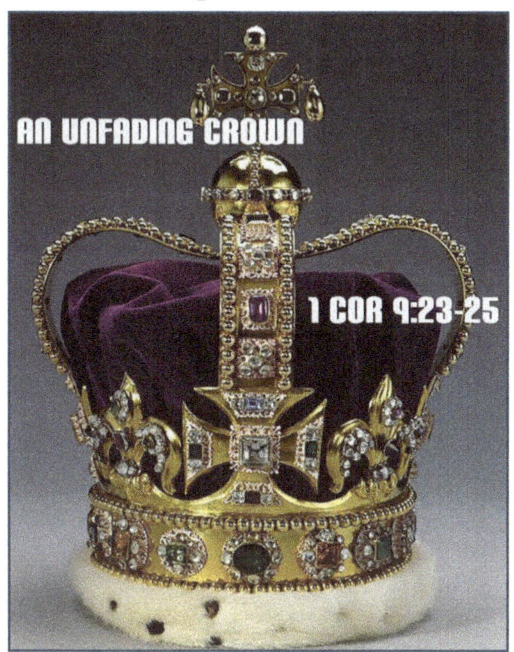

I Corinthian 9:24-25

Know ye not that they which run in a race run all, but one receiveth the prize? So run, that ye may obtain. 25And every man that striveth for the mastery is temperate in all things. Now they do it to obtain a corruptible crown, but we an incorruptible. KJV

Every generation has a similar struggle when it comes to investments. What can I put my money into— that will produce a nice nest egg when I get ready to retire? Some choose life insurance, stocks, and/or bonds, while others choose gold, silver, or diamonds. Some choose buildings, land, and/or businesses. Everyone gets to make individual choices that can make a long-term impact on resources later in life. From the time one is twenty, to the time one is sixty-five, often the financial choices one makes can impact the quality of life, as well as the quantity of saving one has to use. Compound it with years when family is young, or financial valleys or troughs occur, the choices can swing wildly. Of the many regrets that come with the senior seasons, is lost opportunity. For example, if in 1973, a 20-year-old person saves $20 a week ($1,040) a year, by the time they reach 65 in 2018, they will have saved $46,800 in principal. What compounds that savings though is the interest and/or dividends they receive through the years. For example, a savings interest of 1%, would yield $58,740 in the savings account. A life insurance policy yielding 6% would yield, a value of $221,253. A stock fund, that averages 13%, would produce a whopping $1,949,131. The power of interest overtime produces regular substantial outcomes. Unfortunately, most 20-year-olds, don't put twenty dollars a week into an investment plan. In fact, the United States savings rate has been in steady decline for decades. In 1959, it was 11.8% of personal income. As of August of 2016, it was closer to 5.7% of disposable income. In fact, some economists who worry about the future, see due to student debt, credit card debt, mortgage debt, car debt, and regular consumer debt, the rate might be closer to 1% or even negative.

When Jesus spoke to His disciples, He spoke of a different kind of long-term savings program. It was a lifelong investment in the kingdom of Heaven. In Matthew 6: 19-21. He stated, *"Lay not up for yourselves treasures upon earth, where moth and rust doth corrupt, and where thieves break through and steal: But lay up for yourselves treasures in heaven, where neither moth nor rust doth corrupt, and where thieves do not break through nor steal: For where your treasure is, there will your heart be also."* That unfading crown was what Paul was speaking of when called for an incorruptible crown. In another section of Scripture, another disciple, Peter, said each believer should pursue an unfading crown. *"And when the chief Shepherd shall appear, ye shall receive a crown of glory that fadeth not away."* (KJV I Peter 5:4). So how does that work? How do we lay up treasures in Heaven? What does Heaven treasure? As part of one's life regular Assignment, one should be steady, day by day, and year after year invest in heavenly treasure. If a man can compound the interest and turn twenty dollars a week into $1,949,131, what can God do with a lifetime of giving?

Heaven has a value system that is so far different that our world. Heaven values obedience, righteousness, peace, and loving God. When one treasures activities that fulfill those principles, one can lay up Kingdom blessings. For example, in Revelation 5:8, 8:3-4, God stored up Saint's prayers. Someplace, God has storerooms full of the Church's prayers for children, parents, missionaries, pastors, and the needs of brothers and sisters. Also, Heaven stores up tears, David spoke tears in a bottle of Psalm 56:8. When one considers of the shared tears of joy and sorrow over a lifetime, how big is that bottle? Included in a collection of Heaven's treasures are the acts that are meant to relieve the suffering of those one meets in life. Jesus said, in Mark 9:41, *"For whosoever shall give you a cup of water to drink in my name, because ye belong to Christ, verily I say unto you, he shall not lose his reward."* Every Christian should start a Heavenly savings program. It's a crown that will not fade away.

Reflections

- What are you personally investing in that reflects a "heavenly" savings program?

- How can I pray daily that would be worthy of God saving my prayers?

- What acts can I do, like a cup of water, to a child, an apostle, or to a fellow saint, that God would take notice of?

Notes

C

Cecil the Lion

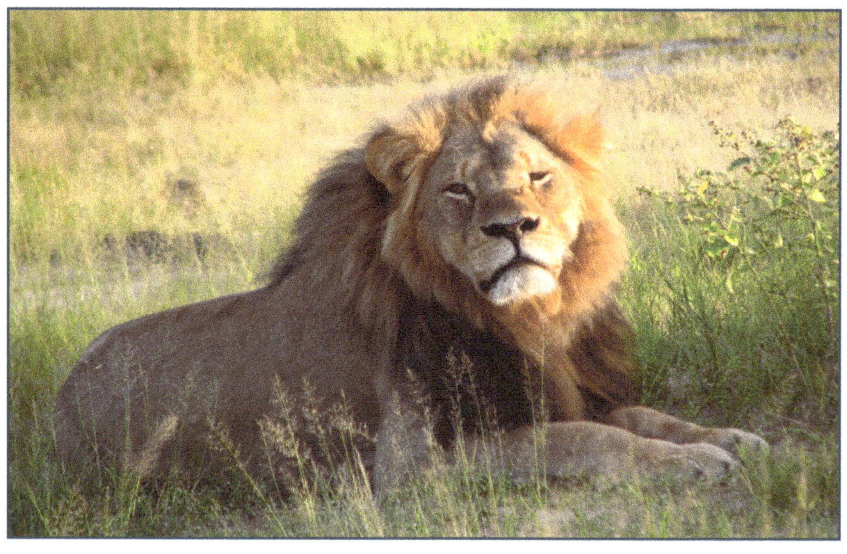

John 1:14

But every man is tempted, when he is drawn away of his own lust, and enticed. KJV

Cecil was a South Western African lion that gained international fame in July 2015. Born and raised in the Hwang National Park in Matabeleland North, Zimbabwe, he was living a comfortable existence with his pride of 22 members. Dentist, Dr. Walter Palmer, who as a hobby was a big game hunter, had paid guides at least $50,000.00 to help him get a lion. The native guide explained how he could get a lion, but he would have to be killed outside of the preserve. So in late June, Dr. Palmer, and his team of natives set out to snare a trophy lion. Near the park's edge, was Cecil and his pride. He had set up thereafter an inter-pride struggle that had killed his brother. Cecil was being watched and tracked in the Park by Oxford University in a 7-year-old conservation study. The guide proved his worth when he used bait to lure Cecil out of the Park safety and into his untimely death. Park officials afterward would discover the grisly remains and begin to piece the story together. The story caught the attention of a number of conservationists, and over 1.2 million signed a petition for justice for Cecil's death.

Out of the many important ideas that resulted from Cecil's death, none is more important than the instruction it gives to each one who walks the Christian faith. This lion died because he was lured out of a place of safety, to a place where his destruction was planned. Inside Hwang Park, Cecil was free to live life as a lion. He reminds us of the power of our own desires. It was some regular, internal urge, that made him walk across a line of safety into the ready gun sights of an enemy. John warned us of the incredible danger a Christian has within, our carnal nature. Even the best of godly examples, still have an internal desire that can lead us to dangerous places. While in the safety of the park, Cecil was protected from evil men. When one's carnality is under the protective influences of God's design, one has a better chance of safety and survival.

God uses several sources to protect us. First, is accountability to God himself. Every Christian should reflect in the mirror about how they are controlling carnality. After being accused of some secret sin, Job protested that in all his soul-searching, he could see where he had allowed his inner man to act in sinful ways. He had done his best to keep his carnality in protective custody. Proverbs 31: 5-6 *"If I have walked with vanity, or if my foot hath hasted to deceit, me be weighed in an even balance that God may know mine integrity."* KJV

Secondly, one must realize that harmful enemies exist that will bring our souls to destruction. Regardless, of our kind, loving, and sincere nature, every Christian has an adversary that would take pleasure in bagging the trophy of our heart and life. Ironically, Peter uses a lion to describe the enemy of our soul in I Peter 5:8 *"Be sober, be vigilant; because your adversary the devil, as a roaring **lion**, walketh about, seeking whom he may devour;"* Just out the gate, is an enemy that seeks our trophy for his wall of shame. Many families, churches, businesses, and lives have been made utter failures because the enemy has a plan to destroy our lives.

Finally, when Cecil crossed the line of the Park, he allowed himself to walk beyond a fence of safety. Fences not only keep people out, but they also protect things within. We can put protective influences in our life, that will help us stay safe. Internet filters, avoiding certain situations, breaking unfruitful friendships, and various other protective means can help oneself. The reason Herod wanted to destroy Jesus as a three-year-old, was so He would never grow to be a King. We need to remove desires and build fences against things that can grow and destroy us at a future date. That means removing a friendship that could lead to improper actions, and avoiding little temptations now, that can grow into bigger problems.

Reflections

- Cecil spent his life in a preserve where he was protected from outside enemies. What are the protections in your life?

- What harmful influences are in your life right now?

- What safeguards is Jesus talking to you about that you can put in your life that will protect you?

Notes

T

Thankfulness

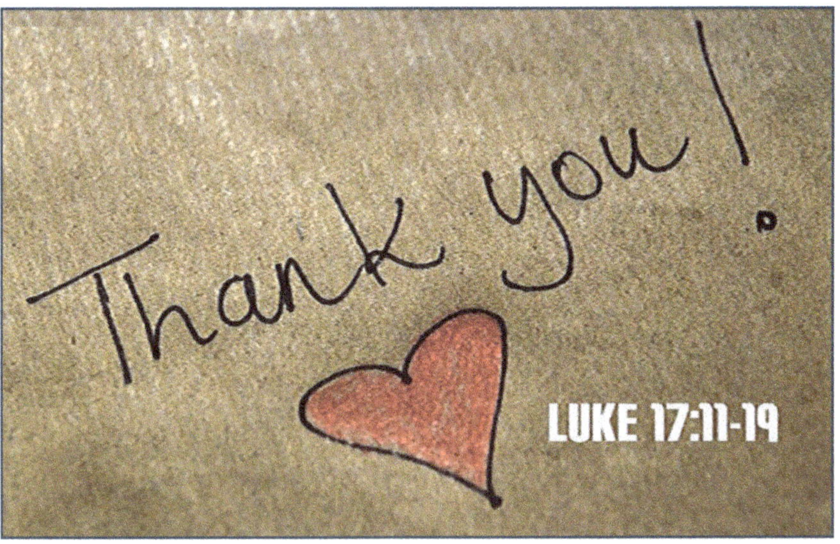

Luke 17: 11-19

And fell down on his face at his feet, giving him thanks: and he was a Samaritan. And Jesus answering said, Were there not ten cleansed? but where are the nine? There are not found that returned to give glory to God, save this stranger. And he said unto him, Arise, go thy way: thy faith hath made thee whole. KJV

Thank-you. A power set of letters that can be defined in so many ways. The attitude of thankfulness should permeate like a sweet cologne in our life. It can be as simple as a nod of the head, a smile, an extended handshake, or even a meaningful sigh. As parents, my wife and I regularly sought to instill this value within our young family. We appreciate even the small acts a child would do. After they would pick up their toys, fold the laundry, or help to clear the table, in our home, we expressed it by saying, "Thank you" or "I appreciate that". Further, after birthdays, and special gifts, we would have Dawn, and Haley, our girls, write out a note of appreciation and hand delivery it to the gift giver. Many have been the recipient of their appreciation; teachers, Grandparents, senior citizens, and other meaningful adults. How long does it take to say, "Thank you!", but so little of it is done?

Luke in his gospel, recounts the story of ten men, who had been healed of a horrendous disease, leprosy. Leprosy separated families, forced isolation, and brought heartache. It mutated their extremities, ears, hands, and feet. The small colony of 10, had gathered as miserable wretches to meager out an existence in the city. When Jesus passed through their village, this day would be far different, because He was going to remove the stigma, that isolated them. Collectively, as a group, they cried for Him to have mercy on them. Perhaps, they had heard of His healing virtue in other lepers. These men didn't waste time debating the particulars. They wanted total and complete healing, and Jesus didn't disappoint them. He still does it today. He touches the hearts of many people, cleaning up a person's soul in a divine moment of healing, metamorphous, and revolution. These lepers went from dirty lepers to clean recipients of love. When Jesus has mercy on modern man, He makes him a brand-new creature. 2 Corinthians 5;17 *"Therefore, if anyone is in Christ, he is a new creation; old things have passed away; behold, all things have become new."* NKJV.

Yet the stark idea Jesus points out is that only one out of the ten return to say, "Thank you". As one by choice, makes his journey back to express his gratitude, Jesus gives him an additional blessing. There is an extra blessing in our life when one gets in the regular habit of acting and saying appreciation. Let's do that for Jesus today. First, by regularly thanking God for the little things that bring us pleasure, amusement, and delight. Spending many moments daily, expressing to God how much you appreciate His hand in your life helping to ease a burden, helping to make a way among many options, and helping to bring relief in stress-filled circumstances. Whisper a prayer of thankfulness for His help.

Secondly, enjoy the benefits of expressing appreciation to others in regular ways. For example, forgetting the negative that clutters our lives working with people. By forgiving offenses, overlooking slights, and washing away rude behavior, one shows they appreciate God forgiving our offenses, slights, and rude behavior. For whom much is forgiven, one owes a lot of gratitude. Also, removing expectations in other's life shows our thankfulness. People get angry, bitter, hurt, jealous, and envious due to expectations. One needs to see how expectations can shape our ideas, attitudes, and actions. "I expected you to have dinner on the table." "I can't believe you acted that way in front of my friends." "If you cared about me, you wouldn't have said that." Too often we let our expectations fill our hearts. How different it is when, with appreciation, one says, "Thank you, for cooking supper tonight." "Thank you, for watching out for me before I made a mistake." "I can tell you care, Thank you." Such gratitude brings a second blessing, from others, as well as within us.

Reflections

- When was the last time, you expressed to the Lord the good things in your life – salvation, your family, or your friends?

- What am I expecting out of others, that is only causing me to angry, hurt, or offended?

- What is happening in the present, that you appreciate the Lord doing?

Notes

B

Brotherhood

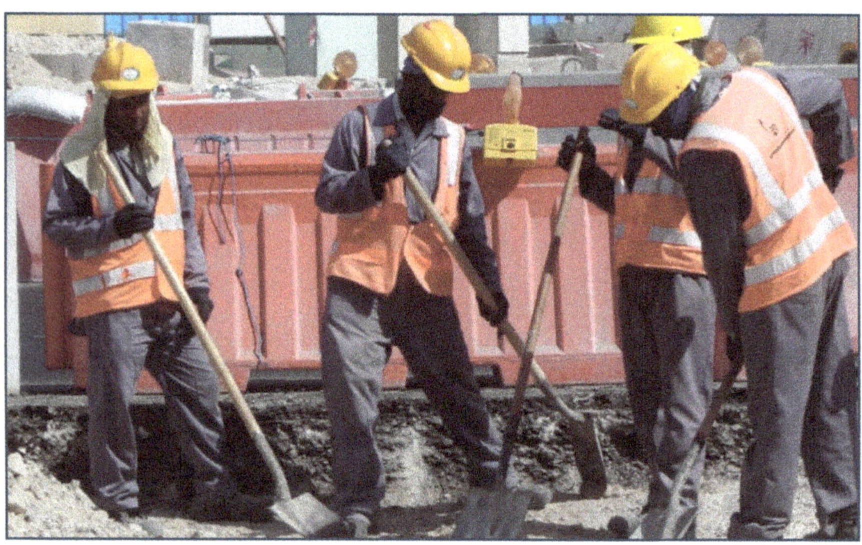

Ecclesiastes 4:9-10

Two are better than one; because they have good reward for their labour. For if they fall, the one will left up his fellow; but woe to him that is alone when he falleth; for he hath not another to help him up. KJV

Brothers come in all shapes and sizes. It is amazing how the same two parents can produce such a wide variety of personalities in one family. Dr. Kevin Leman, in his book, ***The Birth Order Book***, published in 1982, describes the family dynamics that create diverse personalities between the first born, second born, and third. A fascinating study that is accurate by its many observers of the human family. One doesn't have to be related. Solomon is his writing in Ecclesiastes describes how two unrelated people, can develop brotherhood status despite no blood lineage. He is not alone in this understanding. Many groups of firefighters, policemen, soldiers, college fraternities, and various men and women speak of THE brotherhood. A bond that has been forged by life. Its sufferings, and victories. Some single purpose, and life event that forges two people together, in the dynamic of brotherhood.

Solomon describes it quite simply. "Two are better than one." Anyone who has ever walked the course of living experiencing life's curves and valleys may quickly agree. Growing up in a home with seven brothers, I can tell you how true that is. Through the years, I have learned how valuable it is to have a trusted brother even as a defense of another brother. As a young sibling at six years old, when I wanted to learn to swim with my brothers, they said I would have to learn as they did. Eager to join in the obvious hijinks they were up to, I readily agreed. At a young age, I had not learned how to swim, but I knew I wanted to learn. My older brother, Jack, smiled and said, "Okay, here you go!". He picked me up to begin my first swimming lesson. I trusted his strong young arms, my first mistake. I should have realized his method of teaching may include a few panicked bubbles. He quickly launched me into the canal that was located behind our country home. As I fluttered, spit, and sputtered, I hopelessly sank with my young life flashing before my eyes. My other older brother, Brian, quickly came to my aid, bringing me up from the depths of the canal. I was sure at this point, it had to be hundreds of feet deep. While in truth, it was just barely deeper than my young sub-five-foot height, Brian's help in the middle of my crises was a lifesaver. He was just what I needed. He rescued me in the nick of time. Through both of their efforts, I would soon accomplish my desire. Before the afternoon was over, I was kicking, floating, and swimming as we all kicked and splashed in the summer shade--laughing, splashing and goofing off. With a brother, one can accomplish new things in our life.

Secondly, Solomon explains a second aspect. He has designed this life to be shared with others. Why? It magnifies its joys, and bears its sorrows. We hold each other up and give each other strength. In the church, by partnering with another brother of like precious faith, we draw something from each other that opens our lives to new depths, new understandings, and new experiences. Moreover, Solomon observes that there is an exponential reward as two brothers bond together. One person's strength, gains greater, more dynamic strength as we link hearts, heads, and arms. God was expressing this in Deuteronomy 32:30, when he said, "How could one chase a thousand, And two put ten thousand to flight...?" NKJV The reward of laboring together is so much sweeter. When two brothers grab a hammer, a paintbrush, or plan a children's ministry project, the possibility of reward just ratcheted higher.

When one realizes such, rich blessings, one must work to partner with my brother to build worthwhile life projects. Some projects are as simple as spreading the good news of the Gospel. When I stand with a brother of faith, and knock on the door of a stranger, it gives me greater hope for the outcome of each visit. "Who's there?" a question rings out from behind the closed door. I look over at my brother, smile, and say, "The church." As we cross the threshold to visit a shut-in, or to bring cheer to someone experiencing sickness, we have a greater possibility of reward. God helps us to accomplish more together by including others, a brother, and each other to make lasting change.

Reflections

- Who is a person that you would call "a brother?

- What does the relationship dynamic bring to your life?

- What can you do, if you partner with someone this week, that will advance the Kingdom of God?

Notes

H

Higher Level

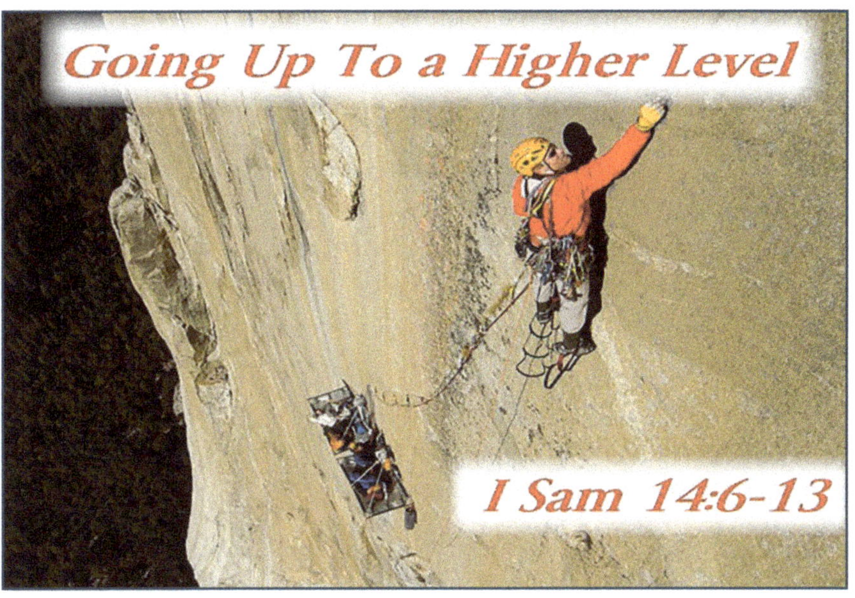

I Sam 14: 6-7

Then Jonathan said to the young man who bore his armor, "Come, let us go over to the garrison of these uncircumcised; it may be that the LORD will work for us. For nothing restrains the LORD from saving by many or by few." So his armorbearer said to him, "Do all that is in your heart. Go then; here I am with you, according to your heart." NKJV

What motivates a man like Peter Croft? Croft climbs mountains, without ropes. Born in 1958, in Canada, Croft has achieved worldwide fame climbing the sheer faces of some of the most challenging rock climbs in the world. He has climbed alone, or in small groups, mountains in Yosemite National Park, British Colombia, and the High Sierra. He even made an ascent on the famed Mount Diablo with its stunning views, but with over 20 kilometers (about 13 miles) of a straight rock climb. In an extreme sport that challenges every muscle of your body, in adverse conditions, as well as taking risks that could easily result in death. Croft is considered one of the world's top ten mountain climbers in the world. He likes going to a higher level.

Jonathan, son of King Saul, didn't like staying on a plateau. He wanted to advance his father's, as well as God's people's nation of Israel in a barbaric and untamed world. The Scriptures tell the story of an army (I Samuel 13) that had only two swords, one in Jonathan's hand, and one in his Father's, and only 600 soldiers against a larger, and battle-hardened army of the Philistines. What motivated Prince Jonathan to climb that mountain? One idea for sure, if he stayed where he was, he wouldn't have progressed any further than he was. Status quo can be a compelling reason to climb higher in life by taking risks. Starting a new business, going back to college, and entering into a new relationship all can have daunting prospects. Yet, it is leaving the comfort that can be an invigorating and intoxicating force.

Yet, a great sense of this particular scripture is the attitude of God's ability. Prince Jonathan believes that God isn't limited by circumstances, situations, problems, or environments. Although, he knew it had its problems, he stated, "…it may be". God works well in the unknown, unusual, and uninviting. That day, turned into a route for the Hebrews. The amazing victory came from confidence in a God who was more than able. Paul summarized a similar feeling about God when he said, in Romans 8:31, *"What shall we then say to these things? If God be for us, who can be against us?"* Why does one fear, when God has no walls, limitations, or fences? God doesn't need swords, armies, or weapons to be victorious. When one has God on our side, the impossible becomes possible. The unthinkable becomes reality, and the extraordinary becomes normal. Two people, six hundred miles apart and with no common ground, can be brought together for an unbelievable romance. A church family with no resources can overcome all odds and see a beautify edifice built in Jesus' name. A job prospect with unbelievable benefits, that seems beyond reach, takes a few steps of extreme climbing in faith, to achieve by a risk taker.

A third noteworthy aspect of this experience of Jonathan was his armor bearer. He didn't have extraordinary faith in God, a sword, or a great army. He simply believed in his leader – Prince Jonathan. God blesses our lives with others who help us climb on their shoulders to new levels. God gifts us these special people to accomplish great things together. His armor bearer had great limitations, but his unshakeable confidence in Jonathan, explains his portion of the miraculous. God will bring people into one's life to help us reach new, higher- heights. Prince Jonathan made the scenario easy for the armor bearer to understand and participate in. By choosing to join in Jonathan's quest, he simply had to follow his lead. As Jonathan climbed between a sharp stone and a smooth stone to the top of the cliff, a young armor bearing was following in tow to a higher level, He joined in the fight, the victory, and the celebration by just following.

W

Whet the Ax

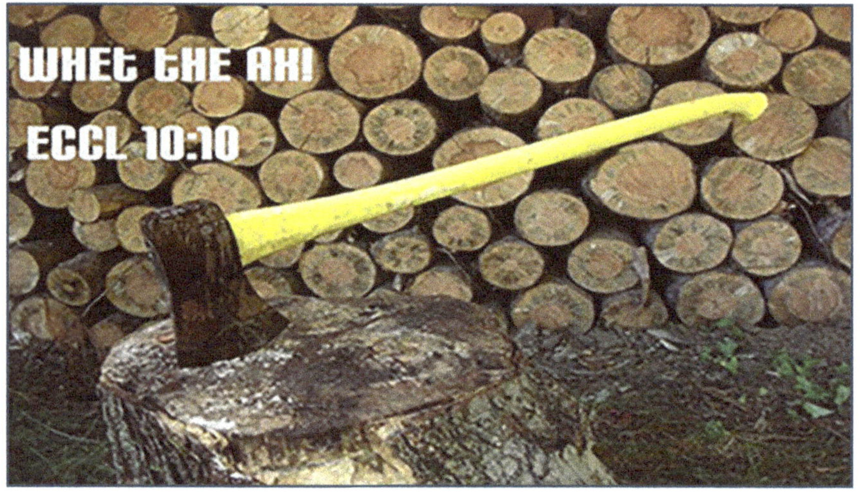

Ecclesiastes 10:10

If the iron be blunt, and he do not whet the edge, then must he put to more strength: but wisdom is profitable to direct. KJV

Solomon gave us his reflections on hard work. In today's world, very few chop wood. If they do, they use a pneumatic wood-splitting machine. The days of using a wedge, and sharp ax are beyond most people. Lost in this old-fashioned necessity for cooking and heating, is Solomon's counsel. He noticed the big job of splitting wood, was made so much easier with a sharp ax. Slice through oak or pine, a sharp ax makes the exertion of strength much less. The closest most modern kitchen aficionados can understand his idea is in the use of sharp knives. In the kitchen, cutting celery, green peppers, and onions is made so much easier with a sharp knife. The duller a knife, the more work that is necessary to expend. Restaurants regularly pay professionals who as a service come and sharpen company knives. Without such service, knives lose their edge. Solomon saw that axes lose their edge and make the job so much harder.

In the course of living, there are three edges that regularly need care in the Christian's life. Chief of which is our heart can get dull. Isaiah 6:9,10, first mentions it, but Matthew also pointed it out in Mathew 13:15, *For the hearts of this people have grown dull. Their ears are hard of hearing, And their eyes they have closed, Lest they should see with their eyes and hear with their ears, Lest they should understand with their hearts and turn, So that I should heal them.* NJKV Wealth, mounds of plenty, and the materialism of our day dulls our heart from the sharp sensitive nature that our hearts, mind, will, and/or emotion need to stay sensitive to the leading of the Holy Spirit in our everyday life. It makes living for Jesus so much harder. One fails to have compassion, do the work of the Lord, and hear the whispers of His call to service. The Lord says, "Spend time with that shut-in." "Take that fatherless child for a couple of hours and spend some bonding time." "Give that one hundred dollars to the Missionary endeavor. Dull hearts make God's work harder.

Secondly, with post-modern thoughts and ideas, our conscience can become dull. It becomes a daily battle on what is right and what is wrong. Conscience is the min-preacher in our hearts that keeps our morality sharp in a constantly moral declining world. Between scientific discoveries, new social mores, and changing expectations of behavior – our moral edge daily needs a whetstone. If I lie, I avoid standing out among my coworkers. If I join in with violations of Scripture, I'll be more accepted. In families, at the workplace, and in social media, our expectations of normal behavior are up-ended into chaos and bewilderment. So, what if I give in to that advance from a co-worker, traditional marriage is changing? Do I tell this white lie at work to get a better promotion? Since I wasn't asked directly by a close friend, can I skirt around from telling the truth? A sharp conscience can make quick work of such dilemmas.

Finally, Solomon pointed out that a sharp ax is profitable; it is like wisdom that one applies to his circumstances. How much better is one's life, when wisdom is put into action? Wisdom teaches one to avoid future problems, by looking over our shoulders to the past. Wisdom points out that every time one buys that bag of chips, a half gallon of ice cream, and a bag of candy bars, the scales scream ouch. So, don't do it. Wisdom says to be transparent to your wife or husband. Hiding things, lying, and willfully acting out, brings out the "beast" in them. So, don't do it. Wisdom will say, put that extra cash in the bank, you'll need it to come winter. Yet, that new set of flats at the local store is crying for purchase. So, don't do it. Listen to wisdom. Keep your ax sharp.

Reflections

- Have I let things God has talked to about go unheeded?

- What things have I allowed into my life that keeps me from hearing God's voice?

- What am I doing today, that is a violation of God's law and/or commandments?

Notes

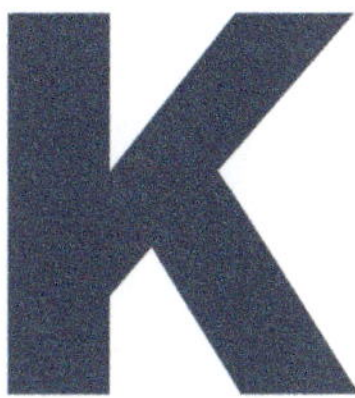

Christmas Kairos

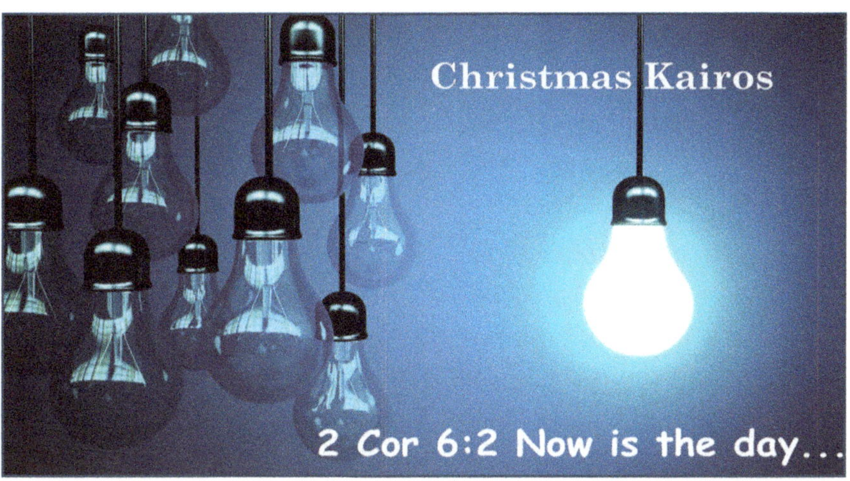

II Corinthians 6:2

(For he saith, I have heard thee in a time accepted, and in the day of salvation have I succoured thee: behold, now is the accepted time; behold, now is the day of salvation.) KJV

Every year, during the month of December, many children and adults experience the Christmas Rush season. It is a part of annual festivities, parties, and family traditions, that have transpired through many generations. Although celebrating on December 25th, annually is a unified, international celebration of Jesus coming into the world, it may not be the exact day, Jesus was born. Some historians have put his actual date into the Spring. For some Scrooges, that fact alone is enough to not take part in the general methods of traditional celebration. Yet, undeniably, He was born at some exact time. A God, indeed, whose miraculous birth, whenever it happened, is worthy to be celebrated. While it seems a grand idea for all of mankind to celebrate it together in many unusual or unique ways, celebrating it specifically is important. Over the years, one can observe Christmas in July sales, or other pre-traditional celebration opportunities. Whenever it was, it was a certain, precise, wonderful, extraordinary, note-worthy event.

Paul in this verse of Scripture speaks of accepted "time". In Greek, he uses the word "kairos" defined as "a fixed and definite time, the time when things are brought to a crisis." It is that crisis that propels an action or event that makes a change. It is this Karios that describes one's salvation. By salvation, he meant a time when one makes a choice to follow Jesus and prepare their heart and life by obedience to do so. Like a light switch that comes on, in each of our brains. It is when a man or woman, brought into crisis- makes a change. They seize the moment to bring everlasting and powerful change into one's life. When did it happen in your life? For myself, it was when I was a twelve-year-old boy living in a small Midwestern town, Ottawa, IL. I can take you to the place where I experienced my own personal crises (Karios) that moved me to the actions of salvation. In a small white church, I headed to an altar to ask God to straighten out the grave problems I saw with my future, hopes, and dreams. Through the years, some have expressed that such a crisis time for such a young man, could not have been that life-changing. Yet, indeed it was for me.

Karios moments enter into our lives when we realize it is a time for action. All the words, creative thoughts, and aspirations mean very little, without action. One could abide in a state of confusion, complexities, or bewildering circumstances, or get an answer for their life. I choose the latter and raised to a small wooden altar and began to weep. Words failed to express adequately how much I needed a change. Like a giant softball in my throat, I had trouble verbalizing the why, or how, but just rather, I wanted Jesus to fix my brokenness. In time, I would be baptized in the name of Jesus, and filled with the Holy Spirit (or Holy Ghost as the scripture states it.) It was my personal Kairos when the lights turned on inside my heart and head.

What events in one's life lead us to make a change? Important days have catalysts to bring us to that point: like the day one decides to go back to school to get the degree, or the day one asks a significant person to join together in the journey of love; or like the day, or even the day, one decides "now" is the day of salvation. Significantly, that particular day, is a crisis point when we seize the day. It is when one comes out of the other side of that internal struggle, our "Kairos", the joy of discovery, and the miraculous are birthed. As one reflects on the meaning of circumstances, events, and directions in my life – each one has a personal Kairos. I often can take you to the place, spot, or location, when I made a bold decision that would change my life.

Reflections

- Can you recall some "Karios" moments in your life?

- What can you do now, to make a change for the good of your life?

- Specifically, what new steps can you take to "seize" the day?

Notes

O

One of a Kind

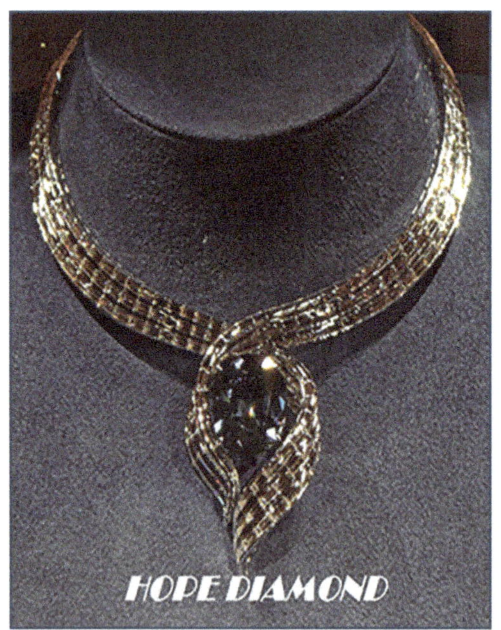

I Corinthians 11:3-4

But I fear, lest somehow, ... so your minds may be corrupted from the simplicity[a] that is in Christ. if he who comes preaches another Jesus whom we have not preached, or if you receive a different spirit which you have not received, or a different gospel which you have not accepted—you may well put up with it! NKJV

One of the most spectacular items that is quite unique is the **Hope Diamond**, also known as Le Bijou du Roi ("the King's Jewel"). It is also called Le bleu de France ("the Blue of France"), and/or the Tavernier Blue. It is a large, 45.52-carat (9.104 g), deep-blue diamond, and now housed in the National Gem and Mineral collection at the National Natural History Museum in Washington, D.C. Originating its view to the public four centuries ago in remote parts of India, the Diamond is insured for at least 280 million dollars. It is one of the most famous, and valuable gems in the known world. It is one of a kind. The rarity, size, color, and complexity add significantly to its value. It can't simply be replaced with another. Two of them don't exist in the world.

In Paul's admonition, one finds his view, that the Gospel message also is unique, extraordinary, and valuable. He warned the Corinthians not to be corrupted by the simplicity that is in Jesus Christ. His concept that love for Jesus and what He represents is one of a kind. It shouldn't be changed, corrupted, or altered from the original character, spirit, and commands that first came on the Day of Pentecost in Acts chapter 2. It isn't the first time; Paul speaks this way regarding the message of Jesus. In Galatians 1:8-9, he reports that to believe any other Gospel would bring a curse to our life. In fact, he says it twice for emphasis. *"But though we, or an angel from heaven, preach any other gospel unto you than that which we have preached unto you, let him be accursed. As we said before, so say I now again, if any man preaches any other gospel unto you than that ye have received, let him be accursed"* KJV Paul's strong feelings should be the feelings and beliefs of every Christian. There are not several gospels, but one gospel. Jude in verse 6, points out that its delivery to the church happened only one time. To contend for it, means to fight for its meaning, concepts, and applications.

Paul even goes on to say, that any other gospel is a false gospel and another Jesus. With tens of thousands promoting religion, gospels, and forms of Jesus, it should motivate one to adhere to the original gospel that Paul was referring to. If in Paul's day, the gospel was being perverted, altered, and re-invented, how much more has it changed since the early church? The solution is to examine the early church in Acts 2, Acts 8, Acts 10, and Acts 19, and discover what was the message preached, believed, and contended for? Quite simply Peter told them on the question of salvation to (Acts 2:38), *"Then Peter said unto them, Repent, and be baptized every one of you in the name of Jesus Christ for the remission of sins, and ye shall receive the gift of the Holy Ghost."* It became a symbol of hope for the devout Jews of his day. Verse 41 says that about three thousand gladly believed and were baptized in the name of Jesus. From that genesis pont, all the other passages in Acts show that hungry seekers of the Gospel followed that sane 3-step pattern. In fact, in Acts 19, the disciples of John were re-baptized to get it right. Paul's question got to the heart of the matter. In Acts 11:15-21, Peter testified that Cornelius' experience was the same as the first disciples.

Through the years, many have tried to falsify, duplicate, and deceive others into believing a second Hope Diamond exists. The imposters have not succeeded to this point. Collectors are not fooled by cheap imitations, bold claims, and fictitious similar diamonds. If you want the real thing, it's one of a kind. The Gospel is the same thing, one of a kind. If you don't have it, you have a fake.

Reflections

- What are the 3 things Peter commands the first disciples to do in Acts 2:38 when it came to salvation?

- In your life, have you followed those same three actions?

- If Paul, Peter, and Jude felt so strongly about the Gospel message, how can we show we are adamant about this distinctive message of the Gospel?

Notes

H

Holy Temple

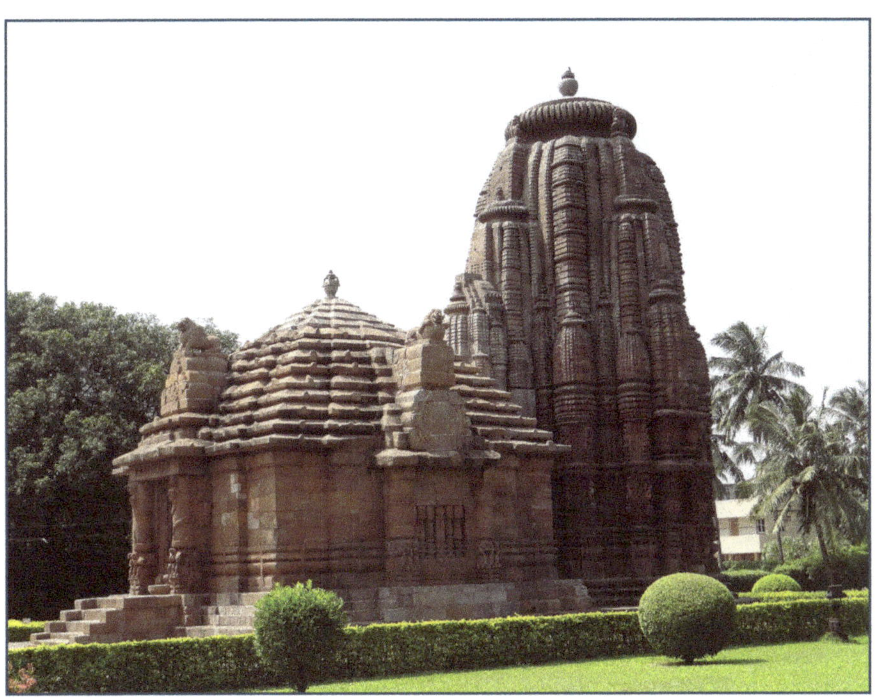

1 Corinthians 6:19

What? know ye not that your body is the temple of the Holy Ghost which is in you, which ye have of God, and ye are not your own? KJV

In America, when a congregation builds a church it is called a church, generally. In many parts of the world, such a building is called a temple. Such buildings are ornate, extravagant, and strikingly unique. Some are dedicated to individuals and others to gods of their choosing. Many have different styles of construction. For example, Gawdawpalin Temple, in Bagan, Myanmar, is a pagoda style. It was built between 12-13th centuries. The temple is used for meditation and other Buddhist rituals. One of the most famous is the Taj Mahal. It is an ivory-white marble mausoleum on the south bank of the Yamuna river in the Indian city of Agra. It was commissioned in 1632 by the Mughal emperor, Shah Jahan, to house the tomb of his favorite wife, Mumtaz Mahal. It was called one of the seven wonders of the world. Some temples are smaller, but just as ornate with stone carvings, and ornamental adornments. Even well-developed nations, like the United States, Great Britain, and the Soviet Union have temples.

The first purpose of a temple is not to show off its elegance, but rather its dedication to life, faith, or memory. The Christian faith was never designed to build ornate structures dedicated to godly zeal, but rather each member of the body of Christ serves as a temple unto the Lord. As a dedicated instrument of God, one is to represent the faith, purpose, and mission of Jesus as reasonable service to God. In Romans 12:1, Paul reminded us of that mission when he said, *"I beseech you therefore, brethren, by the mercies of God, that ye present your bodies a living sacrifice, holy, acceptable unto God, which is your **reasonable service**."* The mission of every Christian is to be a reflective example, through our bodies, of our faith. Can you imagine a temple built like a Mcdonald's? No, because each Mcdonald's is built for the mission of the fast food giant. It is reasonable to be dedicated to the life, faith, and memory of Jesus Christ. When folks see a Christian, are around a Christian, and have experience with a Christian, they should be reminded of Jesus and His hope for their life.

Paul is also, telling the Church member that our purpose is to be the home of the Holy Spirit (Holy Ghost). Where you live, you feel comfortable and act in comfortable ways. One might take off their shoes at the door, but a lived-in home probably has a comfortable chair, a particular design or style of decoration, and/ or unique identifiers of its inhabitants. The Christian temple is no different today. Each of us, is to be in a place where God feels comfortable to live. Many people have visited the home of a special relative, community icon, or special acquaintance. While there, we didn't act like one that lived there. One probably acted stiff, formal, and on our best behavior. I had an aunt who when we visited, she had plastic, clear coverings on her furniture that we sat on. We would sit like angels with our hands politely folded in our laps, our backs against the couch, and our feet on the floor when we visited her. We didn't act that way in our home. We laid down, bent a leg over an arm, and enjoyed life freely. I want the Lord to feel comfortable in my temple. I want Him to relax, stay a while, and not feel a stranger in my mind, soul, and emotion.

Finally, Paul tells us that this temple is a lasting reminder of God's internal and external holiness. One must never forget who owns the Temple. Paul states our ownership is Kingdom minded. A Christian should have deportment that exposes its owner. In I Corinthians 3:17, Paul warns us *"If any man defile the temple of God, him shall God destroy; for the temple of God is holy, which temple ye are."* Destroy is a pretty strong word, but it tells one how animated God becomes when one loses sight of the value of our temple.

Reflections

- How do you show off the elegance, and beauty of God's temple?

- In what ways do you encourage God to be comfortable in your heart, soul, mind and/or emotions?

- Are you involved in any destructive habits that are defiling your temple?

Notes

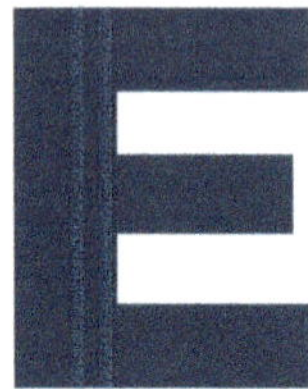

Experience Matters

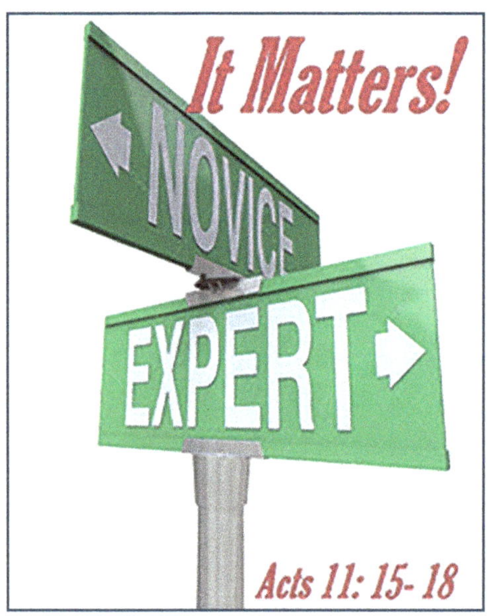

Acts 11:15 -18

And as I began to speak, the Holy Ghost fell on them, <u>as on us</u> at the beginning ...then as God gave <u>them the like gift as he did unto us</u>, who believed on the Lord Jesus Christ; ... When they heard these things, they held their peace, and glorified God, saying, Then hath God also to the Gentiles granted repentance unto life.

The want ad read, *"Mechanic Needed. Knowledge of general engine repair, starting systems, exhaust systems, and electrical systems. Experience wanted."* The employer was stating that he had a good job for someone, but they had to have previous experience in doing the work. Mr. Jeff Fluhr, president of a new method of hiring, (video conferencing with applicants), believes experience is over-rated. He was also CEO of the highly successful internet ticket selling web-sight – Stub-hub. He believes that many more important factors of the job applicant are important. For example, he likes to hire inexperienced people who have qualities that are successful in any job setting, for instance, those who promote good team chemistry, have a likable personality, display a high level of optimism, display above-average creativity, and/or show great intellect. These intangibles are far more valuable, in his opinion than previous experience in the field. Yet, other experts disagree on the wealth of previous experience.

Luke in his authoring of the early church clearly displays that Peter relayed based on his previous experience that the Gentiles too had experienced the same thing that the early founding fathers of the church had. He repeats the phrase *"as on us"*, or *"the like gift as he did unto us"*. The early disciples knew Peter understood what had happened to all of them in the beginning and were confident that he was a ready expert as to the Gentiles experience. Because of that experience, the early church then had credible evidence that God was pouring out the same things that they had experienced. Their confidence swelled, and misgivings fell away immediately.

When does experience matter? Malcolm Gladwell, the author of Outliers, a book on employment, states it matters in three key areas. First, it when an expert is needed, the rule of ten thousand applies. Experts are not newbies, but rather people who have had the same experience ten thousand times. One should have greater confidence in Jesus because the evidence is overwhelming. Especially in this area. Paul in Romans 4:21 states *"And being fully persuaded that, what He had promised, He was also able to perform."* If one has been around the people of God, they are giving the personal experience of a God who regularly, faithfully, and dutifully demonstrates His experience of creating solutions, demonstrating His power, and solving one's problems. Every day He raises the sun -up, puts the moon in the midnight sky, and spins the Earth about its axis. He daily feeds every wild animal, every fish, and controls the wind, the waves, the sea, and the rivers. The evidence of His experience matters.

Secondly, experience matters when one wants to predict the future. It serves as a roadmap for what can take place from here forward. When someone has renovated a disheveled building, framed a new house, or restored order to a chaotic work environment, that life experience is a well from which a repeat performance can be demonstrated. Paul explained that in 2 Corinthians 9:8, when he stated, *"And God is able to make all grace abound toward you; that ye, always having all sufficiency in all things, may abound to every good work;"* If God every healed one's body, delivered one from difficult life dilemmas, or liberated one from unbreakable bondage, it gives us confidence, hope, and faith that He can do it again.

Lastly, experience matters, when it is personal. One cares more intensely about the experience when it's your son or daughter, or your business, or your home. Let someone else be the surgeons first surgery. Let some other clients be the first court case if it means years in prison. Let some other mechanics fix the car, but when it's my brakes, engine, or transmission, only the best, experienced mechanic will do. Our preference is clear when one's interest are at stake. We want only experienced experts.

Reflections

- What is your problem, issue, or circumstance? Is it something God has fixed in the past?

- In your personal life, what are the miracles, providence of God, or sufficiency of His power that you have seen?

- How can you express greater confidence and faith that God can solve your personal situation?

Notes

Inconvenient Request

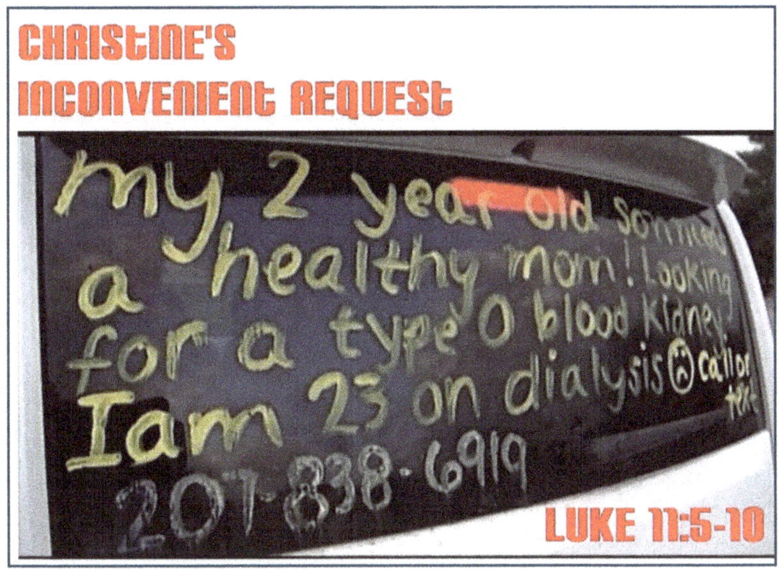

Luke 11: 7-8

And he from within shall answer and say, Trouble me not: the door is now shut, and my children are with me in bed; I cannot rise and give thee. I say unto you, though he will not rise and give him, because he is his friend, yet because of his importunity he will rise and give him as many as he needeth.

"My two-year-old son needs a healthy mom. I need a kidney transplant. Call or text..." It was scrolled on the back window of her Kia Soul hatchback. A request was made by a 24-year-old Mom, Christine Royles, from Brunswick, Maine in November 2014. She was desperate. She was in critical kidney failure and needed to get the word out. She was asking complete strangers for a kidney. Strangers may ask for a meal, a ride, or even a dollar to get by, but a kidney. One is born with only two. As one ages, the kidney function goes down over time. To request a kidney from a complete stranger is more than just a modest asking, but a huge inconvenient request. Desperation can motivate us to do unusual things. When I was a twelve-year-old boy, my parents lost their home due to the inability to pay rent. For a period of over six months, our family of nine was spread among friends and relatives. My pastor and his wife, with four kids of their own, allowed three of us to live with them. It was far from convenient. My parents were left with very few choices. They were homeless and had a bunch of young children. It was either split up the family or be on the street living out of a station wagon. Jesus tells of a story that is not as severe as needing a kidney or taking in a child for over six months. It was simple as a neighbor requesting bread for a house guest. It was behind the backdrop of a day, when getting bread wasn't as easy as a midnight run to a 24 supermarket. The neighbor needed a favor due to a house guest that caught them with no way to feed them. It was simply needing some food as to not embarrass themselves at such a late hour. Jesus brings up this story to emphasize the need for one to keep submitting our requests before God. He called it "importunity": It is persistence; an insistence or demand being met. The fact was, the neighbor was inconvenienced, but he complied with the bread request. When it comes to prayer for our personal needs, God wants us to be persistent. Without doubt, getting out of bed at 2 am is annoying to most people. Yet, for the neighbor who lacks bread, it was completely necessary. He was willing to ask, even if it meant annoying his neighbor. Why do we give up asking God for even the little things that are meaningful? Paul told the church in Hebrews 10:19 *"Having therefore, brethren, **boldness** to enter into the holiest by the blood of Jesus,"* God expects us to boldly enter into His presence and make our requests known – small or great. What could Jesus do for one today? Solve a crisis? Lift depression? Or Restore order to chaos? Just ask. "God, I need you to intervene. Step into this problem and fix it." The man got his bread by his insistence of an answer.

Secondly, the neighbor had plenty of bread to give to his needy friend. It meant getting out of bed and taking care of the problem. The supply was never in doubt. Perhaps, it was the personal knowledge the neighbor had of his benefactor. For example, perhaps he knew that his wife always fixed an extra loaf or two. He simply had no doubts his request would be satisfied. One should have no doubts that God can take care of us. It was Paul who said in Ephesians 3:20 "Now unto him that is able to do exceeding abundantly above all that we ask or think, according to the power that worketh in us," God is able to go higher in abundance. If one needs one hundred dollars, God has ten thousand. He can fulfill our need for strength, peace, love, and hope is easy for Him. One's request is never beyond His ability to supply. So go ahead, and make your request known, it is not like one is asking for a kidney.

Reflections

- Do you have a friend that even if it annoys you, you'd drop what you are doing to meet his or her needs?

- What is one thing in your life, that God could do, that makes your life better?

- Even though God is not a respecter of persons, what does this parable teach us about people who persist in prayer?

Notes

K

King's Table

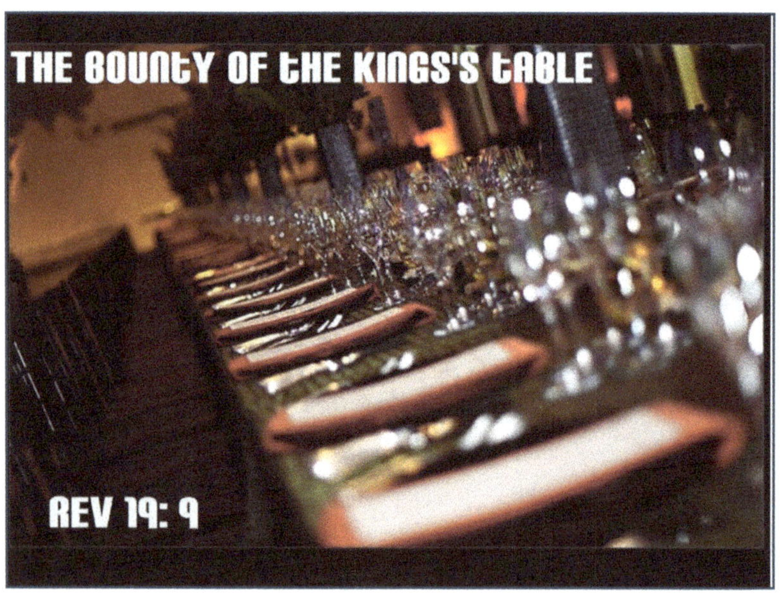

Revelations 19:9

And he saith unto me, Write, blessed are they which are called unto the marriage supper of the Lamb, and he saith unto me, These are the true sayings of God." KJV

The weddings of Jesus' day were far from the weddings of today. Today, multi-million-dollar companies make great profits by making each wedding a media spectacle and an ornate affair. Couples can customize their nuptials with special glasses, table decorations, and a myriad of specialty products. Weddings in Bible days had three major components as illustrated by a number of passages in the Gospels. First, the bride and groom were selected by the fathers of the family to insure proper breeding and a lifetime of providing. After the written covenant between the families, a dowry was paid. What modern couples call an engagement, is the waiting period known in Bible days as the betrothal. Joseph and Mary were in such a betrothal period when Mary was found to be pregnant (by the Holy Spirit, Mathew 1:18). During the second phase, the groom and his friends, (about a year after the signing), would begin a torchlight parade to get his bride. When he gathered his bride and her entourage, they would make their way back to the new home of the couple. This is the basis for Jesus' story of being prepared for the groom's coming in Mathew 25:1-13. The third phase was the marriage supper itself, which might go on for days, as illustrated by the wedding at Cana in John 2:1-2.

All three phases have great parallels to the modern Christian experience. Each has important obligations to the bride and groom. Jesus became the groom by covenantal contract. He paid the dowry of such a bridal agreement with His own blood. Paul explains it in Ephesians 5:25 *"Husbands, love your wives, even as Christ also loved the church, and gave himself for it;"*. It was sealed with His own precious blood ordained before the world began according to I Peter 2:8-10, *"Forasmuch as ye know that ye were not redeemed with corruptible things, as silver and gold, from your vain conversation received by tradition from your fathers; But with the precious blood of Christ, as of a lamb without blemish and without spot: Who verily was foreordained before the foundation of the world, but was manifest in these last times for you,"* KJV

The second phase is when Jesus comes for the catching away of His bride the church, in a parade from Heaven to Earth and back to be forever in our heavenly home with Jesus. I Corinthians 15:50-54 tells of this grand parade. *"Behold, I tell you a mystery: We shall not all sleep, but we shall all be changed— in a moment, in the twinkling of an eye, at the last trumpet. For the trumpet will sound, and the dead will be raised incorruptible, and we shall be changed. For this corruptible must put on incorruption, and this mortal must put on immortality..."* NKJV.

Yet, the third stage is the invitation to the King's table, the marriage supper of the lamb that John writes about that is a grand celebration. The "Called of the Lamb" are His bride and entourage. Each child of God, takes his or her seat at His table where there will be rejoicing and celebration at this marvelous covenant. Unlike a wedding rehearsal that only lasts a few hours, this celebration is unlike any Earth has ever seen. The rejoicing, dancing, and jubilation from the inhabitants of Heaven as well as Earth will exceed our wildest imaginations. We will be blessed of the earth. Distinctly necessary are those who must wear the wedding garment. In Jesus' parable, the invitation was for all who prepare their wedding garment. In Mathew 22: 11-14, *"But when the king came in to see the guests, he saw a man there who did not have on a wedding garment. So he said to him, 'Friend, how did you come in here without a wedding garment?' And he was speechless. Then the king said to the servants, 'Bind him hand and foot, take him away, and[a] cast him into outer darkness; there will be weeping and gnashing of teeth. For many are called, but few are chosen"*

Reflections

- What was the price of the dowry in your life? What did Jesus do to redeem your sins?

- Are your prepared fhor the coming time of Jesus' return? Do you have oil in your lamp? (Meaning is your life a living testimony inspired by the Holy Spirit infilling?)

- What is our wedding garment that is to be without spot or wrinkle or blemish? (Hint: Ephesians 5:27)

Notes

N

Narrow Path

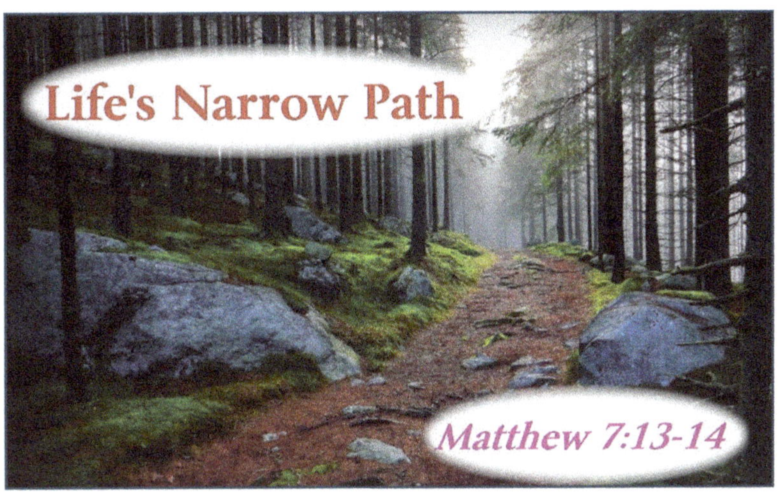

Matthew 7:13-14

"Enter by the narrow gate; for wide is the gate and broad is the way that leads to destruction, and there are many who go in by it. Because[a] narrow is the gate and difficult is the way which leads to life, and there are few who find it" NKJV

Jesus speaks about our own autonomy. One can hear cynics who wish to paint the Christian faith as robots who blindly follow the wishes of the religious few. Nothing can be further from the truth. In fact, it is the exact opposite. Choosing Jesus over the ways of sin is a daily election. Multiple times in a single day, a Christian must make regular choices over the powers and principles of the world, desires of his heart, and deceptive demonic influences. This choice is between the deadly way of sin, or the life-producing way of goodness. Jesus, in His sermon on the mount, touches on this clear fact. Christianity is the ultimate daily liberty. Our choices, methods, and direction are derived from clear decisions on where such things lead us. The simple yellow brick road, the <u>Wizard of Oz</u> might lead the story character Dorothy to the wizard, but the road of faith and trust is not as easy to follow.

The entrance to life starts on a narrow path. By conscious choice, Christians choose to walk an alternative path to the values of the world. In Isaiah 35:8, the prophet explains that course of direction when he said, *"A highway shall be there, and a road, And it shall be called the Highway of Holiness. The unclean shall not pass over it, but it shall be for others. Whoever walks the road, although a fool, shall not go astray."* NKJV In Isaiah's day, following the commands of the Jewish faith was counter to the rest of the modern world. Yet, the grizzled old prophet wanted to convey the importance of Jesus the right way on the highway of holiness. The narrow way is a way that is precise, with a clear value system of Jesus. If one chooses the wrong gate, he'll end up where he doesn't want to be. Like taking the wrong exit on the highway, it can lead you to the wrong location. On the west side of Chicago, there is an exchange that can lead one north to Wisconsin, East to Iowa, South to Indiana, or East to Chicago. Make the wrong choice, and one's end is vastly different. In reality, Jesus pointed out that what is popular may be an unwanted choice. Some gates lead to destruction and the mass of humanity is likely to follow it. Life is like the old TV show, Let's Make a Deal. In it, behind each door was an item. Make the right choice and one got a beautiful car, a lovely vacation, or a room full of furniture. Make the wrong choice, and you got a prize that was a trinket, a gag, or an unwanted and lesser gift. Even with friends and the audience cheering on the contestant, a bad choice ended with a secondary, poor prize.

What a blessing though, to make the choice for the narrow way. Sure, it won't have the glitz, glamour, and bright lights of the world. It will have the glory of the Lord, the sweetness of His Presence, and the companionship of the redeemed. Walking on a narrow path is circumspect. One carefully treads down in a precise, clear, and determined way. I want to walk down the narrow path to life. Isaiah, in Isaiah 30:21, stated *"And thine ears shall hear a word behind thee, saying, This is the way, walk ye in it, when ye turn to the right hand, and when ye turn to the left."* Walking in the ways of God, brings a blessing and it is by choice. As sin is a choice, so is righteous living. When Eve was tricked, Adam willingly followed her into sin. Paul commented on his willing choice when he remarked in I Timothy 2:14, *"And Adam was not deceived, but the woman being deceived, fell into transgression."* NKJV As a son or daughter of God, my choices will determine my future blessings, eternity, and path.

Reflections

- How does my liberty to make a choice determine my path?

- If wide is the gate that leads to destruction, how can I make the right decisions?

- What are the blessings in my life for choosing Jesus over the world?

Notes

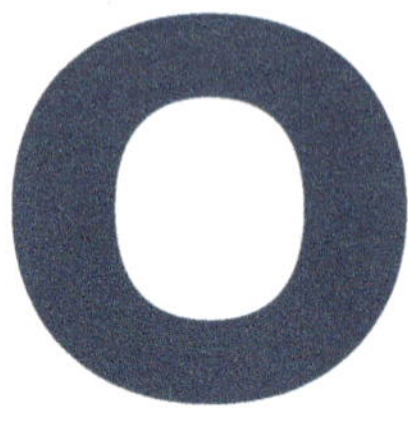

Overcoming Obstacles

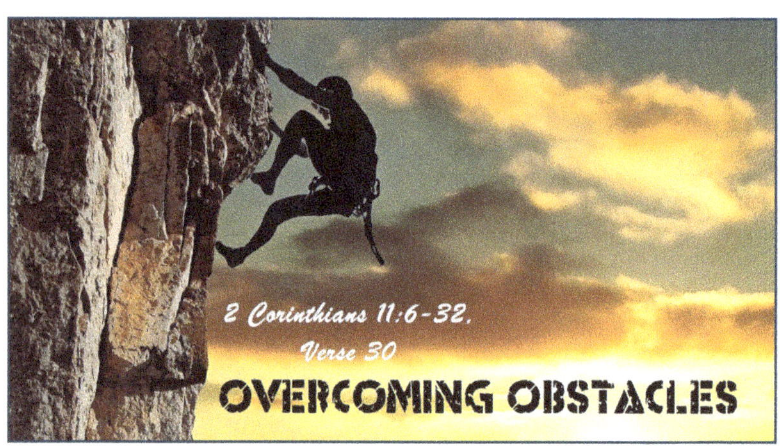

2 Corinthians 11:30

If I must needs glory, I will glory of the things which concern mine infirmities. KJV

Every life that has meaning, purpose, and value will also have obstacles. One may use different words for the things one must endure or overcome, but successful people have them. One can call them hurdles, hardships, handicaps, mountains, hang-ups, interruptions, or hindrances. They are things in our lives that keep us from achieving. What is something in your life that obstructs you or hinders your progress? Paul, in seeking to vindicate his apostleship, begins a list of things he has endured that qualify him to be an apostle. Instead of churches established, souls converted, or great miracles he participated in, he lists the obstacles he has overcome. Paul simply states that vindication of success is directly related to the obstacles one overcomes.

Paul in I Corinthians 11:22-28, lists out the numerous life experiences that marked his ministry. *"Are they Hebrews? so am I. Are they Israelites? so am I. Are they the seed of Abraham? so am I. Are they ministers of Christ? (I speak as a fool) I am more; in labours more abundant, in stripes above measure, in prisons more frequent, in deaths oft. Of the Jews five times received I forty stripes save one. Thrice was I beaten with rods, once was I stoned, thrice I suffered shipwreck, a night and a day I have been in the deep; In journeying often, in perils of waters, in perils of robbers, in perils by mine own countrymen, in perils by the heathen, in perils in the city, in perils in the wilderness, in perils in the sea, in perils among false brethren; In weariness and painfulness, in watchings often, in hunger and thirst, in fastings often, in cold and nakedness. Beside those things that are without, that which cometh upon me daily, the care of all the churches."* He tells each one who wants success, that one has to climb over the problem. In today's world, success is often defined in terms of accomplishments. What a novel idea, to define success in terms of obstacles one has overcome. Great leaders have risen to the top of the success mountain, because they climbed over obstructions that have caused others to fail. Our 16th President, coming from modest means, understood this more than many others. In 1831, Abraham Lincoln failed in business. In 1832, Abraham Lincoln was defeated as a state legislator. In

1833, Abraham Lincoln tried a new business, and failed. In 1835, Abraham Lincoln's fiancée died. In 1836, Abraham Lincoln had a nervous breakdown. In 1843, Abraham Lincoln ran for congress and was defeated. In 1848, Lincoln ran again, and was defeated. Again. In 1855, Lincoln ran for the Senate, and lost. In 1856, Lincoln ran for Vice President, and lost. In 1859, Lincoln ran again for the Senate. He was defeated. Then, in 1860, Abraham Lincoln was elected President of the United States.

What matters most is not how many times you fail, but you keep getting up. Solomon saw this when he remarked in Proverbs 24:16, *"For a just man falleth seven times, and riseth up again: but the wicked shall fall into mischief."*

It was the world-famous Michael Jordan, whose basketball success is well noted. From the time he was a young man, learned the secret to obstacles. He stated, "Obstacles don't have to stop you. If you run into a wall, don't turn around and give up, figure out how to climb it, go through it, or work around it." The great heroes in the Bible listed in Hebrews 11, prospered despite many problems that could have destroyed them. Paul speaks affectionately about them, in verses 33-34"Who through faith subdued kingdoms, wrought righteousness, obtained promises, stopped the mouths of lions. Quenched the violence of fire, escaped the edge of the sword, out of weakness were made strong, waxed valiant in fight, turned to fight the armies of the aliens. Women received their dead raised to life again: n:" His tribute is noteworthy and sums up the critical nature of fighting through difficulties. Our boasting should not be in our accomplishments, but rather in our obstacles.

Reflections

- What are your biggest obstacles to success?

- What can you do to work through your mountains that seem to be hindering you?

- If you think outside the box, what can help you work around the obstacles?

Notes

P

Pen of Scribes

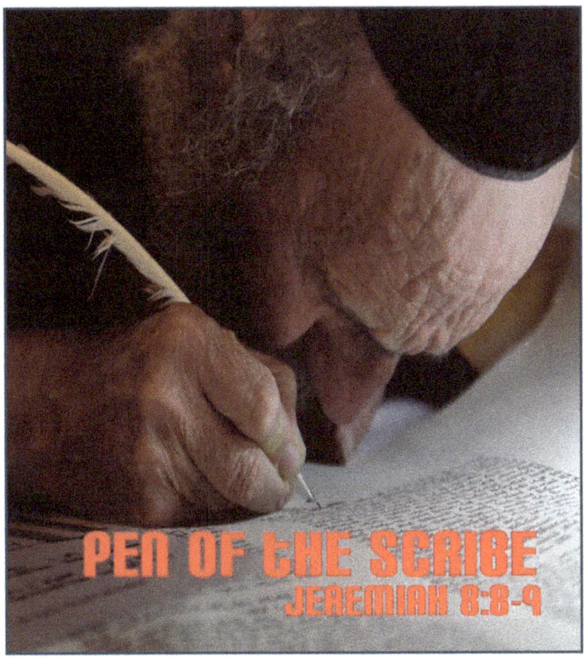

Jeremiah 8: 8-9do ye say,

We are wise, and the law of the LORD is with us? Lo, certainly in vain made he it; the pen of the scribes is in vain. The wise men are ashamed, they are dismayed and taken: lo, they have rejected the word of the LORD; and what wisdom is in them?

Every day America operates with inventions that are a regular part of our lives. It is often hard to think of life without all the amenities that one now uses many times throughout the day. There was a day, not that long ago, when there was no internet, social media, microwaves, smartphones, or high-definition televisions. Yet, life seemed to go on without such technological wonders before they found existence. People fell in love, married, had children, worked full-time jobs, and attended church, week after week. Many inventions, even if the inventor felt them ingenious, have never made it mainstream. Such devices have one's life easier, more connected, and more fully informed. Now, an event can occur 5,000 plus miles away, and we can have pictures, data, and other eyewitness accounts in relative seconds. We have ingested such technology into daily routines.

Here is a passage of scripture, where Jeremiah warns the people of Israel how foolish they have been to not include the wisdom of the Word of God in their daily lives. In fact, Jeremiah concludes that no matter how marvelous the Word of God is, if it is not used, then "the pen of the scribes is in vain". The Scriptures that the church has available to us in more ways than can be numbered are worthless, if one doesn't make it a part of his daily life. Today, the Word can come to our phones daily, posted on our media sites, listened to on CD, WAV files, or anytime night or day. Yet, it has no value, if we don't listen and apply it to one's life. The power of the Word lies in getting it to read. The pens of the scribes that long ago wrote, would be vain, empty, and powerless without readers.

It was Peter, who told us of the origin of the Word in 2 Peter 1:21 *"For the prophecy came not in old time by the will of man: but holy men of God spake as they were moved by the Holy Ghost."* The living Word came to us to be followed. The expectation of God is that we follow His written Word. When the rich man sought to come from the dead to tell his brothers of the horror of Hades, God's response is so telling, Luke 16:30-31 *"And he said, Nay, Father Abraham: but if one went unto them from the dead, they will repent. And he said unto him, If they hear not Moses and the prophets, neither will they be persuaded, though one rose from the dead."* The Word was more powerful than miracles, visits from resurrected relatives, and the supernatural.

Second, the reason the scribes penned the written Word, was God designed for man to have a source of inspiration, encouragement, and blessing. When the great apostle Paul, was in prison, and he wanted comfort, his request was for the Word of God. 2 Timothy 4:13 "Bring the cloak that I left with Carpus at Troas when you come—and the books, especially the parchments." NKJV Paul in the cold, dank, prison cell didn't ask for music, a song, or some memento of his of an earlier time in his life. He asked for the "parchments". Written in the ink on those scrolls were the words of life. Words that brought to life feelings, emotions, and inspiration. Today's Word in its many forms is a tool for all believers to hang tough in troubling times, to bring forth courage when facing fear-filled moments, and to excite the believer in the promises of God as one traverses the wilderness of the modern man.

Finally, the written Word is empty, vanity, without it being shared with another. When the Word is obeyed, followed, and allowed to come alive, it brings a return. It was Solomon, in his wisdom, who observed Word brings blessing back into our life. In Euclasites 11:1, he stated, *"Cast your bread upon the waters, For you will find it after many days."*

$$Reflections$$

- What are the patterns you use to get the Word in your life on a regular basis?

- In what ways do you attempt to follow the Word of God in obedience?

- How can you share the Word of God to someone today?

Notes

P

Pre-Eminence

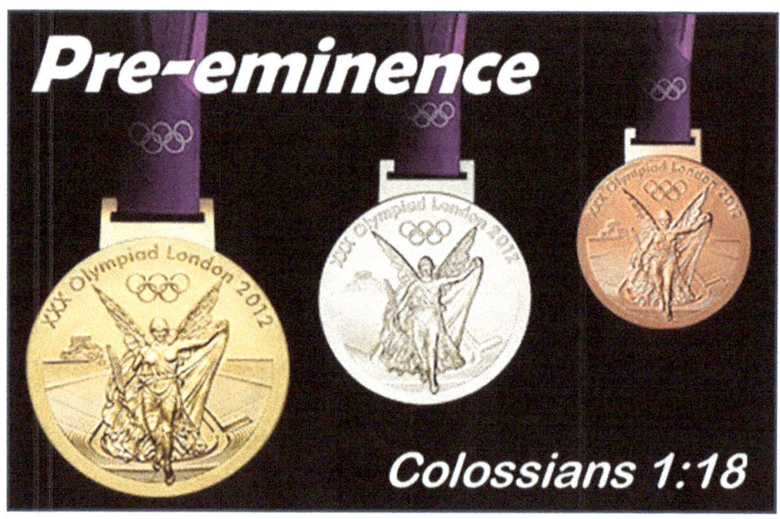

Colossians 1:18

And He is the head of the body, the church, who is the beginning, the firstborn from the dead, that in all things He may have the preeminence. NKJV

In August 2016, the Summer Olympic program featured 28 sports with 41 disciplines, and a total of 306 events, tentatively resulting in 306 medal sets to be distributed. The variety of world athletes was from 87 countries that won medals. 59 countries won at least one gold medal. Yet, it should be noted 120 countries did not win a medal at all. The athletes from the United States dominated the field from around the world. They compiled an amazing record of 121 medals of excellence. The top two countries behind them were China (67 medals) and Great Britain (67 medals). Although, the average American is very proud of their accomplishments, it is a small minority who can personally say they are the preeminent leader in the world, The rare privilege of being among the best is for no less than 121 athletes (a number winning multiple medals in different competitions.) Other fields of discipline have the same result in education, science, and various avocations which have truly few dominate leaders. To be preeminent in any field is a unique set of people. Paul tells the church in Colossae that Jesus should be preeminent in all things meaning He should be above, before, surpassing, and superior in all things. How does one do that?

For that to happen, Jesus needs to be superior in our actions. Jesus Himself, gave us the instruction in Mathew 6:33, "But seek first the kingdom of God and His righteousness, and all these things shall be added to you." NKJV When a child of God seeks the Kingdom first, they make a priority in their actions toward Jesus. It happens by establishing daily, personal disciplines such as prayer, reading of the scripture, and careful life choices. For example, Jesus told of two men, who built their lives on two separate foundations. One foundation, sand, was on worldly values, and systems that shift regularly. The second was on Rock, which represented Kingdom principles. When each had similar storms, only one stood through it all. The one who built his life around Jesus and His kingdom.

Secondly, our decisions must weigh the principles of Jesus versus the principles of the world. As a Christian, one considers the principles of living pure, holy lives for Jesus. Where one goes, what one wears, and how one conducts their behavior fall fully under this spectrum of choices. For example, in Matthew 12:36, Jesus said *"But I say unto you, That every idle word that men shall speak, they shall give account thereof in the day of judgment."* Clearly, He meant for us to weigh words themselves as to whether they please Jesus. A Christian shouldn't swear. Further, our truthfulness will be judged.

A Christian should not lie. Colossians 3:9, "**Lie not** one to another, seeing that ye have put off the old man with his deeds;" Our deeds done in the body, will be judged by Jesus. There are activities a Christian will not do. J.B. Phillips writes of Galatians 5:19-21, *"The activities of the lower nature are obvious. Here is a list: sexual immorality, impurity of mind, sensuality, worship of false gods, witchcraft, hatred, quarreling, jealousy, bad temper, rivalry, factions, party spirit, envy, drunkenness, orgies and things like that. I solemnly assure you, as I did before, that those who indulge in such things will never inherit God's kingdom."*

To put Jesus in the first place of our life, is to set aside even thoughts that are in compliance with Jesus' thoughts. Paul admonished the church in 2 Corinthians 10:5 that we should be *"casting down arguments and every high thing that exalts itself against the knowledge of God, bringing **every thought** into captivity to the obedience of Christ,"* My thought life needs to be in sync with Jesus thoughts for others and myself. If a Christian will let Jesus be first, and preeminent, they will win a gold medal on judgment day.

Reflections

- Are you building your life on the principles of Jesus or the world?

- Evaluate your most important decisions, if Jesus were to evaluate them, what would He say?

- Are your thoughts guarded daily by His Word and Spirit?

Notes

H

Hay Baby

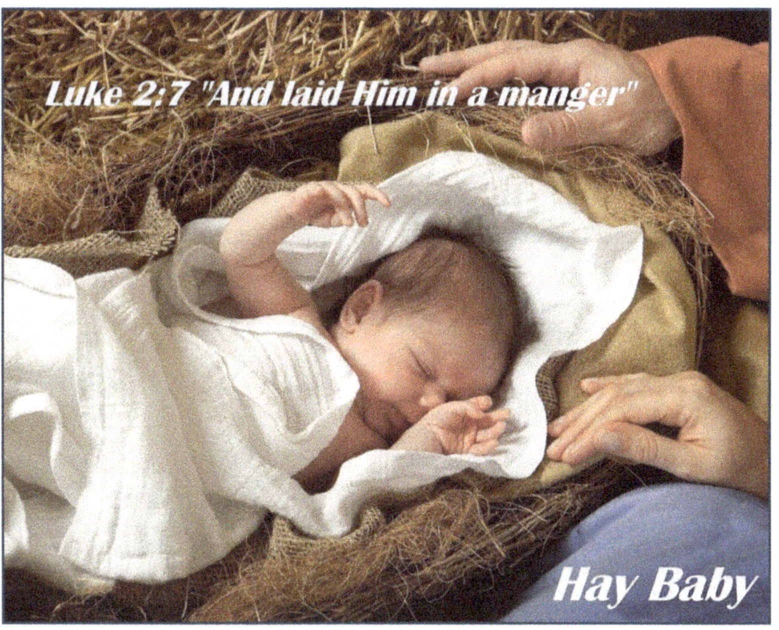

Luke 2:7

And she brought forth her firstborn son, and wrapped him in swaddling clothes, and laid him in a manger; because there was no room for them in the inn. KJV

People around the United States greet each in many different and unusual ways. When two strangers meet, one may hear, "Howdy, sir", "Dude!", "Sup?", "Yo", or even "Hola". On the old Gomer Pyle USA TV show, Gomer was known to give folks a cheesy grin, a wave of the hand, and the Mayberry greeting, "Hey!" Among Christians, there is a variety as well. one might hear, "Brother", "Bro", "Maranatha" and even "Christ is risen!" Growing up among Pentecostals, the common greeting was a simple smile, handshake, and a hearty, "Praise the Lord!". When Jesus was introduced into the world, one wonders how his parents introduced him? If they had been royalty, it could have been quite the affair. For example, Prince William of London, had to discuss his girl (Charlotte) with the good queen's grandmother in person, before it could be announced. In 1982, Princess Diana, 20 years old, had a similar assignment when her proud young father, Charles brought newborn William into international prominence. Yet, Jesus, who was King of Kings and Lords was introduced in a bed of hay, wrapped in swaddling clothes. Swaddling clothes were the rags used to wipe the excess spit from the animals. One could say though, He got a brilliant star, a visit from the Magi, and an angelic choir that lit the midnight sky. This, baby, who was promised many years prior, would have no formality, grandstanding, or celebration parties. He would be introduced to a bed of hay. Why?

First, it would be fitting to His method of earthly dwelling. Paul told the Philippian church that Jesus' early years were profoundly simple, and all men could identify Him as the carpenter's son. It would be a way of life, so He would serve as our example. Christians are advised to live in humility and meekness as He did. In, Philippians 2:5 -8 Paul said, *"Let this mind be in you, which was also in Christ Jesus: Who, being in the form of God, thought it not robbery to be equal with God: But made himself of no reputation, and took upon him the form of a servant, and was made in the likeness of men: And being found in fashion as a man, he humbled himself, and became obedient unto death, even the death of the cross."* The world took little note of Him till His public ministry began when He turned thirty. Prior to that, He lived with an amazing ability that was untapped, and unused till His appointed hour. At the wedding in Cana of Galilee, after the supplication of Mary, His miraculous power of turning water into wine, was on display for the first time. People were amazed even when at the Temple, He told the fellow citizens of Nazareth that *"And all bare him witness and wondered at the gracious words which proceeded out of his mouth. And they said, Is not this Joseph's son?"* Luke 4:22. In fact, His lack of self-promotion, led to some missing out on His ministry among the home crowd. Mathew 13:58 states, *"And he did not many mighty works there because of their unbelief."*

His improbable introduction on a bed of hay, would not in any way diminish His profound role among all men. It was Luke in Luke 19:10 who said, *"For the Son of man is come **to seek and to save** that which was lost."* Belief in Jesus would mean salvation for all mankind, John the apostle would write of His most critical role in John 3:16 *"For God so loved the world that He gave His only begotten Son, that whoever believes in Him should not perish but have everlasting life."* Peter, one of His disciples, would order all Christians to bear His name when baptized (Acts 2:38) for the remission of their sins. Finally, God Himself, would highly exalt Him because of His death on the cross. (Philippians 2:9) What started in a manger would end in exaltation. Rightfully so! That is a wonderful end for a baby who spent his first day laying in hay.

Reflections

- Who is the most important figure you've ever been introduced to besides Jesus Christ?

- Why did Jesus' humility make Him such a great example?

- How did Jesus who according 1 Timothy 3:16, was manifested in the flesh, change the world?

Notes

R
Rejoice

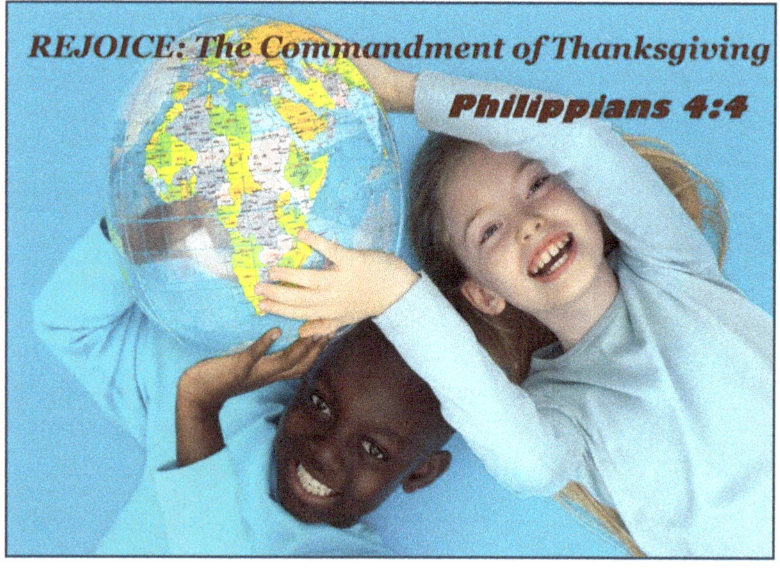

Philippians 4:4

Rejoice in the Lord always: and again I say, Rejoice. KJV

Quite a straightforward command to a people that lived in Phillipi. Rejoice. To rejoice is to be glad or take delight in something or someone. As a Christian, one should learn to take joy or delight in three important conditions of one's life. One should rejoice in blessings, sufferings, and in tribulation.

When one considers how many ways the Lord is delightful, it is much easier to rejoice in Him. First of all, it is God that has granted us liberty and freedom over sin. Jesus has paid the price for our past sins, and for anyone that may come across our path in the future. Paul tells us in Colossians 2:14 *"Blotting out the* **handwriting** *of ordinances that was against us, which was contrary to us, and took it out of the way, nailing it to his cross;"* It is by His cross, that one is made righteous. Paul spoke in 2 Corinthians 5:21 about what marvelous thing Jesus did for each of us, *"For he hath made him to be* **sin** *for us, who* **knew no sin***; that we might be made the righteousness of God in him."* The pure Lamb of God became the scapegoat for my iniquity. It brings rejoicing to one's heart to know that judgment, Hell, and torment are no longer reserved for us, when Christ made us free from its clutches. This great act of love ought to make our hearts skip a beat because He loved us in our most unlovable state. Romans 5:8, Paul explains, *"But God commendeth his love toward us, in that, while we were yet sinners, Christ died for us."* So, let us rejoice in our blessings.

Yet, one can also rejoice in our sufferings. Paul reminded us of a comparison of our sufferings to Heaven's reward. In Romans 8:18, Paul reminds the reader that God is going to shine through us after our sufferings are over. If not in this life, in the life that is to come. *"For I reckon that the sufferings of this present time are not worthy to be compared with the glory which shall be revealed in us."* If we suffer for the sake of His name, one ought to rejoice as the early apostles did. In Acts 5:41, after a terrible beating Peter and the Apostles, found a way to rejoice that they had suffered in the name of the Lord. *"And they departed from the presence of the council, rejoicing that they were counted* **worthy to suffer** *shame for his name."* One also sees another example from Paul and Silas.

After having been beaten with rods, they found at the darkest hour a way to rejoice. It started with prayer and soon the jail cell was filled with loud vocal praise for the Lord. In fact, it was so loud, all the other prisoners heard their vibrant worship. Acts 16:25 *"And **at midnight** Paul and Silas prayed, and sang praises unto God: and the prisoners heard them."*

When one's life has tribulation, it may seem counterintuitive to rejoice, but Paul said to "rejoice in the Lord, always." As one navigates life, so many tribulations can occur; cars can break down, furnaces go out, jobs end abruptly, relationships can go sour, and health can be taken away quickly. Yet, Paul's admonishment is to find a way to dig out water from the well of life's tribulations. Jesus promised us His peace in our tribulations to provide that soul-blessing cheer. John 16:33, *"These things I have spoken unto you, that in me ye might have peace. In the world ye shall have **tribulation**: but be of good cheer; I have overcome the world."* When Paul in Romans 12:12, encourages one to have patience in tribulation, he knew the end result is the entrance into the Kingdom of God. Acts 14:22 reported such an event, *"strengthening the souls of the disciples, exhorting them to continue in the faith, and saying, "We must through many tribulations enter the kingdom of God."* God opens the door of blessing when tribulations darken our life.

It doesn't matter the conditions one finds himself in, Paul's words are a command to follow: Rejoice.

Reflections

- What are the blessings of God you have in this life?

- Paul and Silas started with prayer when enduring tribulations; are there sufferings in your life to pray about?

- What areas of your life do you need more of God's peace in?

Notes

R
Rejected

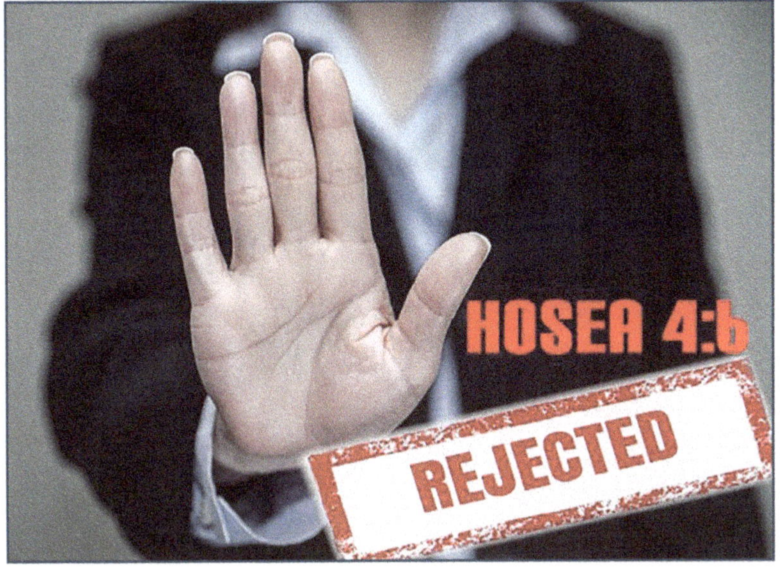

Hosea 4:6

My people are destroyed for lack of knowledge: because thou hast **rejected** knowledge, I will also reject thee, that thou shalt be no priest to me: seeing thou hast forgotten the law of thy God, I will also forget thy children.

Rejection can be a powerful motivator and de-motivator. When one considers the various avocations that regularly deal with rejection, one might consider salesmen, writers, inventors, and job applicants. Rejection can be both a daily mentor and an enemy at the same time. It can cause one to dream big, and lose hope just as quickly. People can use many coping techniques to handle rejection. For example, one young lady, after twelve dates in a row, left her with unrequited love, her attitude was amazing. She smiled, and said, "I tell myself, that is one less fish in the sea. Now, I'm closer to finding my dream boat. You have to decide who is worth your tears and who is not. I just move on." Others, let rejection immobilize them from achieving in life. Consider the great writers who suffered a rejection that later became a great literary achievement. C.S. Lewis, *The Chronicles of Narnia*, L.M. Montgomery for *Anne of Green Gables*, J.K. Rowling, *Harry Potter*, and even famous cowboy story writer, Louis L'Amour for *Banter*. Rejection is often a symptom of good or poor judgment. There is one rejection that leaves no doubt. Hosea, a prophet expresses the Lord's opinion, of Israel's poor judgment of His Word. Because they rejected the Word, He, therefore, rejected them as well.

Hosea expressed that without the Word of God, Israel was destroyed. The Word of God is the stabilizing force in one's life. Without the Word, Israel exposed itself to the destructive influences of sin. The apostle James warned the church left to our natural impulses without the Word, one is led to his own destruction. James 1:13-18 *"Let no man say when he is tempted, I am tempted of God: for God cannot be tempted with evil, neither tempteth he any man: But every man is tempted, when he is drawn away of his own lust, and enticed. Then when lust hath conceived, it bringeth forth sin: and sin, when it is finished, bringeth forth death. Do not err, my beloved brethren."* Our error comes when one doesn't observe the fences the Word of God brings into our life. David observed the Word gives us guidance against enemies of our soul, when he penned the words, in Psalm 110:11, 42 *"Thy word have I hid in mine heart, that I might not sin against thee... So shall I have wherewith to answer him that reproacheth me: for I trust in thy word."*

Secondly, God has left no choice, but to reject those who reject the Word. He is bound by His own Word. When one rejects the laws of God, he is rejecting God himself. It is with certainty that God has to reject those who don't follow him. The disobedience that one has to His law, forces God to reject us.

In Galatians 1:6-9, for example, God rejects those who don't follow His gospel exactly as he has laid it out for man to follow. *"I marvel that ye are so soon removed from him that called you into the grace of Christ unto another gospel: Which is not another; but there be some that trouble you, and would pervert the gospel of Christ. But though we, or an angel from heaven, preach any other gospel unto you than that which we have preached unto you, let him be accursed. As we said before, so say I now again, if any man preaches any other gospel unto you than that ye have received, let him be accursed".*

When mankind makes a misjudgment, one can simply move on, and that rejection is not fatal. Rejection of the Word of God is a spiritual error that one can't move forward from. Adam's sin invited judgment for many generations after him. Paul reminded us how the disobedience of Adam affects all the sons of Adam in Romans 5:12, "Wherefore, as by one man sin entered into the world, and death by sin; and so death passed upon all men, for that all have sinned:" Instead of rejecting the Word, one needs to follow the Word, which brings blessings into one's life.

Reflections

- In what ways, have you rejected the Word of God?

- How does God judge one's disobedience in this life and in the life to come?

- How can one turn back the clock when they recognize they have disobeyed the Lord? (Hint: Psalm 119:11)

Notes

S

Soldier

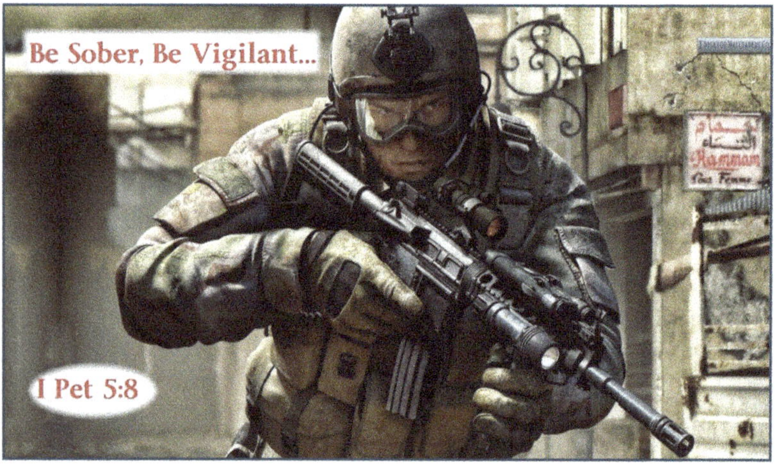

I Peter 5:8

Be sober, be vigilant; because your adversary the devil, as a roaring lion, walketh about, seeking whom he may devour:

The Honor Guard, who are stationed in Washington, DC, at the "Tomb of the Unknowns" (Unknown Soldier), have brought tears, and sobering respect for the fallen American heroes to many Americans who have observed its pageantry. Built in 1921 to honor an unknown soldier brought home from France. It entombs him in a three-level marble monument that millions have come to observe. The highly detailed honor guard has come to symbolize vigilance, respect, and duty. Dressed in his finest blue garment, the guard steps off 21 steps in his walk across the tomb. He hesitates for 21 seconds and does an about face to return his walk. With white gloves that glisten in the afternoon soon to prevent the dropping of his grip on his rifle, the marine guard moves back and forth. Guards are changed every thirty minutes, twenty-four (24) hours a day, 365 days a week. Since its creation about 525 soldiers have guarded the national memorial dedicated to soldiers, and have inspired men, women, and children around the world to be vigilant.

When Peter reminded the church to be sober and vigilant, he reminded the church that we have an adversary. An adversary is simply an enemy, an opponent that stands against the present and future of the child of God. Peter's instruction was for us to be vigilant. He meant to watch out for our enemy. He meant for us not to fall asleep but stay awake on guard for his devious tricks and destructive influences. It would seem nothing seems to represent the importance of such duty like that of a soldier. A well-trained soldier is cautious and pays strict attention to his surroundings. The last thing any soldier wants to do is fail to recognize the enemies' presence. An acute awareness is what Paul warned Timothy, the young preacher when he said in 2 Timothy 3:1, *"This know also, that in the last days perilous shall come."* Paul would recognize our day when events, circumstances, and clarion values should make us awake to what the enemy is seeking to do in our lives and the lives of people we love.

A second thing that Paul would see about a vigilant soldier is that they would have to stand against destructive forces that could overwhelm one. He also told Timothy in 2 Timothy 2:3, to *"Thou, therefore, endure, as a good soldier of Jesus Christ."* Soldiers are not snowflakes, that melt during a tough battle. They are rugged, trained, national heroes that fight for their country and ideals. As Christians, who fight under the banner of Jesus Christ, we must be *"strong in the Lord".* (Ephesians 6:10) and . We must not be weak, confused, bewildered, and running scared in the sound of battle. Being sober is a calm, collected assurance that we are representing His cause, His purpose, and His Gospel against a relentless enemy.

In that same passage to Timothy, Paul points out the third idea in verse 4, *"No one engaged in warfare entangles himself with the affairs of this world.* We can't get distracted. The captain of our salvation, has included us to be the finest, fighting force of generations, The Japanese attack on Pearl Harbor didn't come out of the blue as some portray. There was abundant evidence of an imminent assault. Japanese communications had been intercepted hinting at the time of the raid. A 19-year-old Army private, Joseph Lockard, thought something was wrong with his equipment. The enemy couldn't possibly be attacking, he would later tell others he had thought as he sat on a hill high about Honolulu. The adversary is using a full, all out, attack to distract Christians with a culture war in music, movies, the internet, and social media. Don't get caught off guard.

The best news of our Lord's command, is that if we stay vigilant, one day, we will win. Paul reminded all of us in Romans 8:37, the children of God come out as the winners, *"Yet in all these things we are more than conquerors through Him who loved us."* One Jesus showed us the way to victory if the church stays awake.

Reflections

- What has been the thing that you would admonish other Christians to be trapped in today's culture?

- What battles have you fought and won? How has God prepared you to win in the future?

- Chosen to be in this army, in what ways can a Christian stay strong and sharp in resisting the enemy of our soul?

Notes

Title	Page	Source
An Unfading Crown		https://www.pinterest.com/pin/452048881320459213/
Cecil the Lion		https://upload.wikimedia.org/wikipedia/commons/1/1e/Cecil_the_lion_at_Hwange_National_Park_(4516560206).jpg
Thankfulness		http://i1.wp.com/idealistcareers.org/wp-content/uploads/2015/04/thank-you-note.jpg?fit=1000%2C699
Brotherhood		http://l4.yimg.com/uu/api/res/1.2/1kwmCc05y4wCX4vIW1IGRg--/aD03MDQ7dz0xMDI0O3NtPTE7YXBwaWQ9eXRhY2h5b24-/http://media.zenfs.com/en_us/News/afp.com/Part-NIC-Nic6514815-1-1-0.jpg
Higher Level		http://hdphotohub.blogspot.com/2011_05_01_archive.html
Whet the Ax		http://www.firewood-for-life.com/splitting-axe.html
Christmas Karios		https://sheroes.in/img/uploads/article/high_res/business-opportunity.jpg
One of a Kind		https://upload.wikimedia.org/wikipedia/commons/3/30/Hopediamondnewset.jpg
Holy Temple		https://upload.wikimedia.org/wikipedia/commons/9/9b/Rajarani_Temple_2.jpg
Experience Matters		https:// images.megapixl.com/3849/38498874.jpg
Inconvenient Request		http://www.verdadegospel.com/adwp02/content/uploads/2015/04/kidney-donation-AP-Photo-WMTW-TV_-Kevyn-Fowler.jpg

King's Table		https://jackschull.files. wordpress. com/2011/02/kings-table.jpg
Narrow Path		https://www.walldevil.com/wallpapers/ a85/thumb/9639-forest-tree-path-rock. jpg
Overcoming Obstacles		http://1.bp.blogspot.com/-raqIj__zfPU/ U1W2ha9hLwI/AAAAAAAAUfM/ B640o YRJGXI/s1600/ Overcoming+Obstacles+ Message+Series. jpg